STARVE THE MONSTER

A Powerful Process To Kill Your Addiction Thinking

Hugh Quigley PHD

Published in Great Britain in 2017
Under the **HypnoArts™** label by
the Academy of Hypnotic Arts ltd.
1 Emperor Way, Exeter, EX13QS

AcademyofHypnoticArts.com

Enquiries should be addressed to
the Academy of Hypnotic Arts.
bookpub@hypnoarts.com

First printed edition 2017
British Library Cataloguing in Publication Data
ISBN Number: 978-1-9997641-1-1

*This book is dedicated to ALL my teachers.
The first of these are and were my Parents Big Hugh
and Ann. They say that children are a gift, my parents
were my gift and also gifted me with Helen, Paula and
Tony.*

*Moving through life inspiration hits us from different
angles, my deepest hit was from Dr Fran Renwick.
When all else had fallen away she acted as a scaffold
for me.*

*There comes a point when we get to look in the mirror
and become our own inspiration. Do that for yourself
and deal with your Monster.*

CONTENTS

A special note about how this book was created

This book was originally created as a live interview. That's why it reads as a conversation rather than a traditional book that talks "at you". It's also why it isn't after an award for literature but, it will engage, educate and empower you

I wanted you to feel as though I am talking "with you", much like a close friend or relative. I felt that creating the material this way would make it easier for you to grasp the topics and put them to use quickly, rather than wading through hundreds of heavily edited pages.

So get ready to Starve the Monster and kill your addiction thinking.

Sincerely,
Hugh Quigley

Introduction

Jon: Hi everyone and welcome to: Starve
       The Monster covering Ending
       Functional Using especially for
       Professionals but as with all of our
       experts works if you want to enhance
       your experience of life, then there will
       be advice and techniques you should
       know and will benefit from...

       This is Jon Chase for HypnoArts and
       today I'm talking with addiction and
       recovery Expert Hugh Quigley about
       what Professionals, who use, need to be
       successful with getting their life back

What is Starve the Monster?

Jon: Welcome Hugh!

Hugh: Hi…

Jon: Okay, Hugh, so in a short sentence or two, what is Starve The Monster?

Hugh: Well Jon, Starve The Monster is a process I've developed over 10 years of working with people who have been dealing with substance abuse issues.

It evolved as a process to help people identify what was actually going on in their mind.

Jon: Where does that take them?

Hugh: It takes them to a place where they
         begin to understand that they've given
         control over to something inside of
         their own mind, which we call the
         monster.

         It's easier to identify it as a monster
         and to be able to identify that monster,
         and how it keeps getting them to feed
         it, to make it stronger, to actually give
         it what it needs, as opposed to what
         they really need in their lives.

Hugh's Story

Jon: So, tell us, Hugh, how did you get here?

Hugh: How did I get here, Jon? Oh, that's an interesting story.

I struggled with alcohol in my young adulthood and into my adult life because the monster kept giving me excuses, telling me things: that I was anxious, I was socially anxious, I was incapable of doing things, I was stupid, I wasn't smart enough.

So in order to deal with all of that going on inside my own head, I started to use alcohol.

In using the alcohol, all I did was feed the monster.

I actually fed that monster to a point where I had to take action myself, do something about it, and change my behaviours.

That has helped me develop, understand, work with people who were **functioning,** and are *functioning in their lives*, but are **feeding the monster** when they come off duty.

Jon: Tell me, Hugh, and this is always a hard one to ask people, but tell me what actual impact did it have on your life?

Hugh: It stopped me from developing my abilities. It *slowed* down my understanding.

One of the things that we have to remember when we use any substance, be it alcohol, be it drugs, is that the frontal lobe of the brain, the part that actually helps us look at the consequences of our decisions, switches off a bit.

Therefore we are not able to *think* about the consequences of doing this or doing that. We end up the next morning with **foggy brain**. We're not functioning properly during the day.

We think we're brilliant and we're doing absolutely wonderful, but we're only functioning at a very very small part of our potential because part of the brain has been switched off by the substance.

The **monster takes control** in order to be fed.

Jon: How did that, particularly in your life, affect you. Was there, and there usually is, I know, was there an epiphany point?

Hugh: There came a point where I just had enough, and I couldn't go on with life through the cloud of the alcohol.

Basically, that's how it was. It took me to a very dark place of depression, chronic depression! Then from that, I realised I can't do this anymore.

Once I stopped using the alcohol and started building my life, I made decisions for education, I made decisions for career, and successfully have done so over 27 years.

Jon: I know you told me that you left school early, and then went back. What age was that?

Hugh: I left school at fifteen and a half years of age with absolutely nothing, no GCSEs, no A levels, absolutely, not even a certificate.

Then went to the local technical college and tried to accumulate stuff, but I wanted to get out and work. If I got out to work, then I would get money, and then I would be able to go out partying.

It's basically what I did. Then my epiphany for education came in the late '80s.

In the late '80s I made a decision that it was time to do something different. Got great support with that decision, and from that moment to this moment, I haven't stopped.

Jon: Do you have a specific story, Hugh, that you can share with us of how it actually affected you on the ground, something that maybe our readers, our listeners, could resonate with and say, "Yeah, well, that's me."

Hugh: Okay, Jon, I think a significant story would be where I let the *functional* drinking turn into *dysfunctional* drinking and where I ended up in a hospital ward in a coma for three days in my early 20s.

People would say, "Well, that's an epiphany moment. Why did you not realise after that?" I did, for a while, but I didn't see that the problem was the alcohol.

I didn't see, through the cloudiness,

through the monster talking to me, it gave me a break for a few months, but then I slowly got back into it again.

From that moment on, things began to change.

I saw I was getting back into the pattern again, and that's when I realised, "I don't want this anymore." I don't want this monster controlling **my life**, taking over and telling me what to do in order that it could be fed.

What's going On?
A commentary on
professional using

Jon: Hugh, with all due respect, you're not
        16 anymore. You're not even in your
        early 20s anymore, and the world does
        change.

        I know that alcohol has been a big
        problem, drugs is a big problem,
        especially as we were talking before we
        did this interview on drugs that people
        take because they think they help them
        function, and function better,
        amphetamines and things like that.

        So what's going on right now so the
        professional users need to end
        dysfunctional using even more now
        than they did before?

Are there any specific areas, for professionals who use, that you can see where things are going to get shaken up, have a major impact, or even change the future?

Do you see things staying pretty much where they are for the foreseeable future, or is there going to be a big change?

Hugh: Over the past number of years, unfortunately, the pattern of use has increased.

Drugs seem to have become a part of the fabric of society, that this is what people do.

On their Wednesday evening, they'll have something, be it alcohol, be it another type of substance. Then Friday night, they look forward to Friday nights, Saturday nights, and how they can cure on a Sunday so to return to work on a Monday, knowing that on a Wednesday...

I've seen that pattern increase. I've seen people go from what they call functional, they needed it to relax after work and the functional use stage, where they thought they were in control, turned into dysfunctional use.

I've seen families fall apart. Yes, there has been an increase in use.

The thing about it is, which is really really interesting, these people are in professional jobs, professional careers, have the potential to move up the ladders in the arenas that they work in, and yet, they're stuck.

They think they're stuck because they don't have the right qualifications, or they don't have the right skills, or the manager is doing this to them, or the CEO is saying no they're not the right person.

They don't realise that part of their

stuckness is the reality of what they're doing, the using, be it alcohol, be it drugs.

It's clouding their ability to think in a way that's clear, that they can make the decisions that will get them on that next rung of the ladder, that will take them into the next qualification within their career, and will eventually give them something that they have worked for.

I've seen a **growing** awareness that drugs are very much a part of socialising and very much a part of life.

I've also seen a growing awareness within ourselves, within professionals, that people are becoming more and more and more stuck in the pattern of addiction thinking, and they don't see it.

The impact of killing your addiction

Jon: What's the impact of killing your
         addiction thinking on people's
         existence, especially on a personal
         level?

         We know it's going to impact their
         career levels and potential, but how's
         it going to affect them?

         If I kill my addiction thinking,
         fortunately I'm not in that position,
         but if I kill my addiction thinking,
         what's the impact?

         What impacts have you seen,
         obviously not saying any names, but
         what's the impacts that you've seen
         where people have killed their
         addiction thinking and really found

something else?

Hugh: What I've noticed when people kill their addiction thinking and starve the monster is that they have a **freedom** and a **freshness** for life.

They begin to realise that things that they were stuck with, that they thought they were stuck with, where they thought, "Oh no, it's everybody else's fault," they begin to take responsibility for their lives and they begin to take responsibility for the results.

I've watched people from 16 to 65 go out and do things they'd always wanted to do, young people actually choosing the career that they wanted.

Might not be the career they stay in, but actually clear headedly making a decision to say, "This is what I want to do now."

Whereas up to that point, they were

faffing about, or whatever you want to call it, they weren't clear headed.

There's a lot of faffing about that goes on when there's drugs and alcohol involved.

I've seen older people that felt they were stuck at home because they were using herbal cannabis or they were drinking too much and not feeling that they could go out and socialise, actually turn their lives around, become parts of clubs, **do things**.

One lady decided to go skydiving. She was 68.

All because she was stuck behind the bottle and she couldn't think clearly about the things that she wanted to do in life.

The looks on people's faces when they realise they can have the life that they want if they choose to make decisions that aren't to feed the monster.

What causes functional using to get out of hand?

Jon: I know I'm going to get partially an emotive answer here, partially a scientific one I'm sure, but what causes functional using?

We all know functional users. We all know people who are in positions where they're obviously functional, but, especially career professionals and you and I have both dealt with doctors and people like that who let the functional using get out of hand.

What causes the functional using to get out of hand and go to the next level and become dysfunctional?

Hugh: How it changes? It changes on different levels.

It changes on the brain level, where the people become used to the drug creating the high, creating the buzz, so the dopamine levels in the brain change and they become reliant on the substance in order to create the feel good factor.

Physically the organs of the body also become dependent on it. Therefore the body becomes flooded and so requires the substance in order to function.

This is the belief of the monster as well.

Then psychologically there is that sense of dependence that "*I can't function*".

The belief system, the addiction, the monster thinking, whatever you want to call it, the monster convinces the person that without the substance they cannot function properly.

And at one level the monster is right.

That's why we have to be very careful when we're working with people that have gone from function to dysfunctional use.

Jon: At what level is it right?

What happens in us that addiction actually becomes part of us, that we actually do need this stuff?

Hugh: There comes a point of tolerance in the body where people start using small amounts, and then ever increasing amounts, until that point where the body can't function without the substance.

So that's physically, biologically, and behaviourally.

It affects all areas of their life.

The brain has changed, we know that, we've just talked a moment ago about the ability to think about the consequences of our actions. **That** goes.

Because the people use in the evenings or on the weekends, they think that there's no carry over on to the next day. Of course there is!

It affects everybody in different ways. We have to be very clear about the individual.

When we get to that point where we recognise that the substance has taken over, that the monster is now controlling our systems, **then** we have the whole idea of, "Yeah, the brain is now not producing the dopamine that we need in order to feel good, so we have to put this substance into our body."

Jon: So it affects our ability to create the good chemicals that we need?

Hugh: Very very much so, Jon. It takes over

the dopaminergic system.

Where we would naturally produce dopamine, that's why we wake up in the morning and we need to eat to produce the feel good factor chemicals, we reduce those as we go through the day.

Then we get melatonin, which allows us to sleep at night.

There's this constant process that's going on in the brain and going on in the body.

If you put something else in that interrupts that system, then the system begins to rely on that chemical because the brain has the ability to switch off.

It also has the ability switch on, that's why we starve the monster, that's why we challenge the addiction thinking.

The whole process, it's looking at how it's affecting all areas of our lives and what we need to do in order to reestablish that balance, that homoeostasis that already exists in the brain. How do we bring that back into sync..

What can we do about it?

Jon: I know we're going to get into your actual process that you've developed and that you've used **successfully** thousands of times.

But can we have a synopsis of that? What do we actually do about this?

Hugh: First of all, you have to learn, you identify what we're talking about here, that there is a monster that you've fed, that you've planted a seed.

That monster is now growing and it's got control of your life.

Step one. You can give it a name. You can say, "Yes, this is my cocaine monster."

Or you could say, "This is my alcohol monster."

Whatever it is, you can then look at the whole idea of what feeds this monster.

What is going on in me that feeds this monster?

Do I believe, which is addiction thinking, do I believe that I need this to function? "I can't relax without a line of coke."
"I can't relax without a bottle of wine." This is the type of thoughts that the monster gives you.

That is the **addiction thinking**.

Then it's learning to replace all of that and look then at the emotional drivers that go behind that, because that's what the monster loves: to push your buttons.

It loves to say, "Oh sure. You're okay,

it's grand. Are you bored? Have a line. You're excited? Have a line. Are you making friends? Have a couple of pints."

Whatever it is, the monster will use whatever is in there in order to drive you to feed it. Then we look at the whole process of what do we, as individuals, need to do in order to work with the monster?

That's the rough outline, basically, of what happens.

What are the alternatives?

Jon: So if starving the monster is the
         answer, and I know, we're going to
         show people that it **can** be, what are
         the alternatives? Let's face it, Hugh,
         we don't want to slam anybody
         because people in the business of
         helping people are in the business of
         helping people.

         But, what are the alternatives that
         people are looking at that might not
         have the effectiveness? That they end
         up coming to see you at HURT or in
         your private practise?

Hugh: For many years now, we know that
         the *AA model,* the *12 step model* has
         been about.

         That's a model that's based on
         powerlessness. Now that was

appropriate in the 1930s when it came about.

It was appropriate that it came out of the medical model. Which the medical model determines it's a disease.

That's okay for those, for those people who need that. I think it's important to say that there are people who go to the point where it does become an illness, and we need to be very aware of that.

There are models out there that work for those. There are lots of other different approaches.

You can go into rehab now and begin a psychedelic treatment in order to come off drugs and alcohol, and you can come out clean, sober, whatever.

There's many many ways that we can do it, this is just one model that I have find and developed that works for people.

So, yes, there are many models out there, and many ways, and I would have people come to me who have gone through the other models.

I'm like the last resort, I'm like the last hope that they can get their lives turned around. That's what I work with.

Jon: Okay. You mention that it becomes an illness?

Are you saying that the body becomes so traumatised, so impacted, that it becomes sick? That's a whole different ball game, isn't it?

What point does the addiction become, like for yourself, a life threatening illness?

Hugh: I think it's when we get to the point that we constantly feed that monster.

As we constantly feed the monster, because of whatever beliefs that are going on that the monster is using to get us to feed it.

There comes a point where the body becomes polluted, totally, the organs, the muscles, our brain becomes so dysfunctional that we need to, then, look for different help. We need to look at a different way, and that's where the medical model comes in.

That's where detoxification in a proper medical centre comes in, and in some cases that's what I have to do. I **have** to refer the person to medical detox. I need to work with their GP sometimes because they've let it get to the point of dysfunction.

They've **lost** control. They're **dependent** on it physically as well as mentally.

The mental bit, the psychology bit, yeah, we can work with that, but unfortunately, or fortunately, I don't know which one, I'm not trained to work with the physical detox.

Jon: So, would you say that your drive for this work, and for one thing to get out there, was to get people before they get to that point?

Hugh: It would be **absolutely** brilliant if we could get people to recognise where they're coming to that point, where it's moving from function, they can actually function, and we need to be very aware here and very careful.

They're functioning through a cloud, they're still having the effects, the hangover, which as we know a hangover is a detoxification of the body, so they're still having all of that, so we want to get them at the point before it may even get to there, and they realise that life can be different.

Their existence can be much more greatly expanded before it even gets to

31

the dependency stage, the dysfunctional stage, where it has taken over their lives, destroyed their family, emptied their bank account.

We have hundreds and hundreds of those stories.

What's the right mindset for reclaiming your life?

Jon: Let's move on to the actual process.

          Before we do that, what's the right mindset for a professional or a career person, or business person, or anybody else who might be reading this, listening to it who uses, what's the right mindset for them to be in when it comes to getting started with reclaiming their lives?

Hugh: It's really interesting when people ask me that question.

          Do you have to want to do it?

          I think what they need to do is want to be in a position where they want to sit down and talk to someone about what's going on. It's taking responsibility and saying, "Yeah, I just might need to talk about this."

Whether they make a decision to engage in a process, that's neither here nor there. I think it's the willingness to be able to sit down with someone, or read this book, watch this webinar, whatever it is, and recognise, "I need to take a different step. I need to take a different course of action here."

It's about being able to just recognise within themselves, "Yeah, I just need to talk about this." Talk to a friend. Talk to your GP. Talk to whoever, but it's first of all recognising that you might be functioning in your life, you might be moving up the ladder, but you're doing it at a *cost* to your own **mental health** and your own **physical body** through using substances as an excuse to relax.

Jon: It's back to the old, you've really got to

want this.

Hugh: Yeah.

I think there's a step before that. I think there's a step of recognising that change needs to occur, and then making the decision, do I want to do something about it.

I would have people come to me, they're not even sure they want to be there. It's a conversation, "What brought you here? What do you want to talk about?"

"Well, I just want to talk about what's happening." "Okay, let's talk about it."

There might be an uncertainty, there might be a lack of wanting to come up to it. There might be fear, "What's my life going to be like if I stop this?"

All of those questions are worth just

chatting out, talking about. Nobody's saying you have to do it.

That's not what it's about. It's about the idea of recognising, this is doing something to me and I want to sort out whether I need to change my behaviour. Simple as that.

The desire to want to do something about it comes after.

1. Name the monster

Jon: So let's get into the process. What's the first step?

Hugh: **First step** is being able to **recognise** and **name the monster**.

That's being able to look at your life, at what's happening in your life, and turn around and say, "I have grown a monster here."

It could be a *wine* monster. It could be a *beer* monster. It could be a *cocaine* monster. It could be a *methadone* monster. It could be an *ecstasy* monster. **It's still a monster.**

The first step is actually **naming** the monster, knowing that this monster, this alcohol, drug, whatever monster, is **controlling** you to a certain extent.

Jon: If someone's stuck doing that, what can they do to get unstuck, to actually call it out and say, "My monster is X."

Hugh: Do you want the honest answer?

Jon: Yeah.

Hugh: **Just name it.**

All they have to do is look at their behaviours and recognise that they're having their two or three bottles of wine five nights a week, and just say, "it's the wine monster."

It's there in their behaviour.

How many times do they go to the drug dealer? *How many times* do they go to the off licence? *How many times* do they go to the pub? *How many times* do they meet up with friends for drinks? *How many times* after work do they meet up, or just go for a quick drink before...?

All they have to do is look at their behaviour. The evidence is there.

Look at their bins, **what's in the bin?**
How many little packets of ..?

Jon: And of course, it might not be social
either, might it? It could be using
something privately that the rest of
the world doesn't know about.

If the rest of the world does know
about it, is it worse? I'm looking at
this from my point of view, although I
don't use anymore, but would it be
worthwhile to say to people you
know, like and trust, "What do you
think my monster is?"

Hugh: You'd have to explain to them what
you mean by the monster.

I think a better question is,
"Do you think my drinking, or do you
think my drugging behaviour has
gotten a wee bit too much? How do
you find me recently?"

Which then just seeks to confirm that
they're identifying that something is

wrong with themselves and just
looking for extra evidence to say,
"Yeah, this has become a problem."

Jon: You're naming the monster, obviously,
because you're saying,
"Do you think my drinking's a
problem?"

Hugh: Yeah.

2. *It is external to you*

Jon: What's the second step? Step two.

Hugh: **Step two** is to recognise that it's external to you.

The substance is **external** to you.

It is something that you go and buy. You go to the super market, you go to your local drug dealer, you rang them up, you can bring it in, and you go through the ritual of actually feeding the internal monster, the psychological monster that's driving you to do it.

It's basically looking at what am I doing.

First of all we've named it. It's the alcohol monster, it's a drug monster. Then we have to recognise that that's external to us as well.

That it's something outside of ourselves that we actually go for, we

41

do something in order to get it, so that's the external part.

That is the actual drug that creates the monster inside of the brain.

I say drug, but I include alcohol when I say drug because alcohol is a drug.

We need to be very aware of that. It's a legal one, but it's a drug. Be very very aware of that. Don't say, "Oh, my friends use cocaine, but I only use alcohol." You're still using a drug, the reality of it is.

Being able to ***externalise*** that and put it out there and say, "Well I did go to the supermarket and buy the three for 15 pounds, or the three for 10 pounds, or I buy a lovely bottle of bubbly at 35 pounds."

Whatever it is, it doesn't matter, it's external to you. What we're starting to do there is put the monster outside of our selves.

It's **in** there. It's **in that substance,**
and it's something you reach for, it's
something you buy, and maybe drink,
or you snort, be real about it.

It's external to you.

3. *Monster talk*

Jon: Once we've named the monster, we've put it outside of us so that we can see it and we can look at it. What's the third step?

Hugh: **The third step is where we go internal.**

We go inside our own head and we look at the monster talk, and how does your monster speak to you.

How does your monster tell you that you need to use? We said a wee bit about this earlier, it's about the whole idea of what feelings, what emotions, is there trauma there in your past? Is there something that the monster will use inside of your head to get you to actually go external, get the substance, and take it in to feed the monster so the monster can have more control of your life.

It's basically learning to understand

monster talk.

Your monster, it's different for
everyone because everyone has had a
different experience, so the monster
could actually be using,
"I'm sure you're a user, so it doesn't
matter, just get on with it."
Or, "You're not going to get up the
ladder, you're not going to move up
into management. You're not going to
become a CEO. You're not going to
open your own business."

Despair, hopelessness, powerlessness,
all of these things, whatever it is that
you choose to run as a thought and as
a feeling is what feeds the monster.

All of that, you can call it negativity if
you want, I just call it food for the
monster.

Any experiences that you're using to
stop yourself from moving on, the
monster will jump on them because it
just wants to be fed. It's about taking

responsibility and noticing what the monster uses in order to drive you forward to go external, buy the substance, and then take it.

I think a really good example would be the movie *Little Shop of Horrors* from many many years ago. A meteorite falls out of the sky, lands in a florist's office and it starts to grow.

What it needs is human blood. That's what it needs. That monster had to be fed, so it convinced the person to actually get it what it needed, otherwise it was going to have other consequences.

That's just like the monster inside of our heads. It will tell us we're going to go into sweats, we're going to be feeling sick, we're not going to be able to feel good, we're not going to be able to relax or switch off.

It will use **everything** in order to make sure that you go and you get that substance in order to feed it.

It's constantly saying, "Feed me," but you have to *learn how it speaks **"feed me"** to you.*

It's beginning to understand what is that pattern in your head, what are your excuses, and they are excuses, to feed the monster. Be real about it. It will **use everything** and **anything.**

Should you stub your toe, it's, "Oh, my toe's sore, I'll sit by and I'll do this," whatever. It's all of those sorts of things. It will use any excuse, because remember: **it's growing and it's getting bigger.** The bigger it gets, the more it needs, the more food it needs.

You go from maybe one or two nights a week, to three or four nights a week. Three or four nights a week turns into five or six nights a week. Then before you know it, you've got to the stage where you can't live without it. It controls you completely.

Jon: All right. I had to smile when you mentioned *Little Shop of Horrors,* because when I was at school, I actually played the plant. The line "Feed me. Feed me now," is looking deviously.

You're saying that's what it's like.

Hugh: Yeah, that's what it becomes.

Jon: And to listen to the language that's in use. Okay. Do you think, then, that we learn to ignore that rather than listen to it?

Hugh: I don't even think it's a process of learning to ignore it.

I think we just accept it for what it is. We rationalise and we justify without even knowing that we're rationalising or justifying.

They say,

"I've had a hard day at work. I'll sure stop off at the dealer and get a couple of grammes of coke and I'll chill out tonight."

Or, "I'll just stop off and get a couple of bottles of wine on the way home. That's not going to do me any harm."

This whole rationalisation process, this **addiction thinking process** that goes on that the monster will use any excuse.

I can't get that across strong enough. **The monster speak is a key factor to understanding what is driving you forward to actually use the substance.**

So be aware of all of your excuses. It will use **every excuse, every reason, every thought** or **feeling** in order to be fed.

4. What's really happening?

Jon: The next step, what's the fourth step?

Hugh: **The fourth step** is, we mentioned this slightly earlier, but it's important to actually **recognise it for what it is**, it's what do you do, what steps do you do, what steps do *you take* in the process of using.

What actually happens?

Do you get a thought or a feeling? Do you then get up off your backside, go and get your car keys, go to the pub or go to the off licence. Do you go out, send a text to your dealer, "I want, whatever"?

It's being able to identify that it's an actual behaviour that you engage in because you have to go and get the stuff.

If you don't get the stuff, you can't use it. If you don't get it, the monster's not going to be fed, but it's the uncomfortableness that people go through, that they don't want to go through, that sense of "If I don't have my couple of bottles of wine, if I don't have my drug whatever, then I'm going to feel uncomfortable."

Yeah. We all feel uncomfortable in lots of situations. That's part of life.

This is something that we'll all pass. The process of using is literally a **behavioural process** that you go through based on how the monster has convinced you that it's time to use.

This is where the steps all start to come together, where you start to be able to recognise the monster speak, know that it's the monster speaking, and maybe do something different, maybe not, it's your choice.

Jon: How long does this step take, because I know people will be saying, "Oh yeah, that sounds easy."

But obviously, just saying, "No, not just now," isn't going to work.

On average, how long would the reader, the listener, expect to have to change the behaviours before they become a new behaviour?

Hugh: It depends on how much they want the outcome.

If they have a goal, if they have a target, if they have an outcome that is more precious than the use, then they'll do whatever it takes to get that outcome.

If they want to move up the ladder and become a manager, or become a CEO, is that strong enough to drive the new behaviour to actually move forward? It depends on each person.

It depends on how much they believe the monster has control and how much they think that they want to believe that the monster has control.

If they listen to the monster speak continuously, that ain't going to happen, because the monster's going to give them excuses to use.

Whereas if they have a very clear outcome, very focused on what they want, where they want to go, how they want to live their life, what their existence, the word you used earlier, what their existence is going to be like when this monster's no longer controlling their behaviour, no longer controlling their family, their relationships, no longer controlling their bank account, and **above all**, and this is important to professionals who use, it's not blocking their career, because it does get in the way of their career.

I don't care what they say, it does sabotage their career. If they want a monster that they can starve and stop feeding, to continue to have an excuse to stop their career, then go for it.

Make your choice, but know that you're doing it. Whereas you can learn, and in a very very quick period of time, how to starve your monster, your particular monster.

Jon: Apart from obviously maybe physically impacting people, the people that we're aiming to get to, how long, on average, does it take? I'm going to put you on the spot here.

10 days, 15 days, 20 days, three weeks, six weeks, 10 months?

Hugh: Everybody's different. Sorry, but that's just it.

Jon: Obviously, so give me an average.

Hugh: Right. Okay, on average I would work with people between six and 10 sessions, which is 50 minutes a week for six weeks or 10 weeks. That's the average.

Some people get it quicker, and they realise, "No, I can do this on my own. I've got the principles. I can move on."

They then work the programme themselves. They work the model and the process themselves so they can take it forward. Other people might need that extra bit of support.

Now again, we have to be very careful, and I know you said this Jon, but it's important to realise, it depends on **how strongly** the monster has taken over the person's mind, and particularly, their body.

If medical intervention is needed, then we have to include that as part of the programme. But while the doctors doing their bit, the medical doctors doing their bit, we're doing our bit as well so that we reduce the possibility of relapse.

It's all about *moving forward*.

Jon: So would you say, if nothing else, running this process and thinking about this process and going from naming the monster right through to the next bit, if nothing else, that can put you into a position where if you need medical help, you can go step forward and say, "Hey, I need help."

Hugh: Yep. It's a programme which gives you back control of your life. It's a process that allows you to follow each stage at whatever time in your life you're at, in order to turn around and say, "**I want my life back now,** and this is what I'm going to do in order to do it."

It's that commitment, it's that understanding, that allows the person to take the next step in the process. If medical help is needed, so be it.

If it's not, even better.

5. Starve the monster

Jon: Okay. What is the fifth step of your five step process?

Hugh: **The fifth step,** and we've mentioned it right the whole way through, and it's the name of the book, it's *starve the monster.*

During the previous four steps, we've learned the necessary tools, techniques, understandings, and above all, awarness's, levels of awareness of what's actually happening.

For the person who goes through those first four steps, they're at the point where they're actually starving the monster.

The monster is getting smaller. It does diminish because you're not feeding it. If you don't feed something, it fades away.

Let's be real, let's be practical about this. If I go on a diet, I'm going to get smaller, so this is the same for the monster. The same principles apply.

Therefore, it gets to that point where it becomes a distant shadow, a distant memory that no longer controls you because you have taken full control back of your life.

The whole process, the last step is literally putting it all together and ***starving the monster.***

Jon: One thing you said to me prior to the interview, when we'd been talking as well, which I think we need to mention here, is that you said that people were scared of giving something up, but they're not giving something up, they're actually gaining something.

Just purely on a practical level, and I'm sure people, most people will know the science involved in this, but sort of like if I'm used to large amounts of alcohol, I'm use to large amounts of drugs, even nicotine and whatever, how long before that stopped having an effect on me that feeds the monster without my emotional input?

Hugh: I keep coming back to this. It's different for each one of us.

It depends on how strong the hold has been on each one of us. It depends on how strong the monster talk, how loud the monster shouts, and it's working in such a way that our level of awareness gets greater and greater with each day, with each moment that we begin to recognise that the monster is talking to us.

If there's medical intervention, say for example there is physical dependency, or some level of physical dependency, then we need to work with medics on that as well too.

Usually after 72 hours the body has detoxed. It takes those three days for the body to go back to a sense of balance.

The liver has done what it's needed to do.

You've been exhausted through the process, physically, because the liver needs to do that. It needs to get the body clean, that's what it's job is.

For each and every one of us, it's working with yourself, it's working with the plan, it's working with the model in order to say, "Where am I today? God, I don't feel really too well," so maybe you do need to go and speak to a pharmacist or go and speak to a GP.

It's about taking responsibility for putting your life back in order. That's what it's about.

How long is a piece of string? I don't

know, it depends who's cutting it.

I think it's really really important that we recognise that for 72 hours after we stop using, we are going to feel like crap. We're going to feel awful.

You're going to have the sweats, you're going to have the diarrhoea, you're going to have the exhaustion and the tiredness and the wanting to lie on the couch and people to tend to you. You're going to have that.

But after those 72 hours, the body begins to come back to a clear state of balance.

And it's that clear state of balance is the goal, now then a different process occurs.

Because you've moved from the physical crapness, the physical awfulness to another psychological bit.

This is where the monster will want
to get you to use after that third day.

It's about being able to look at, "Well,
what is the monster telling me?
What's my monster speak? What's the
monster talking to me about? Oh, this
or that."

All of that, and if that's when you
take a different step, the physical has
happened, you've stopped it.

You've done everything you need to
do to physically detox, and remember
we're talking about the functional user
here. We're not talking about the
dysfunctional user. We'll come to that
at a later stage and another book
possibly, but at this minute in time
we're talking about the functional
user, the person who can go ahead
and have a life or lifestyle while using
a substance.

When you stop using the substance,
it's usually 72 hours. That's when it all

occurs. That's when this process, the five steps, the five stages really come into effect because that's when you work with the monster.

Mistakes, Myths and Misunderstandings to Avoid

Jon: Hugh, that sounds wonderful! It actually does because when you boil down all the systems that I've heard before, and as you know, I've been in the business, like you, a very very long time, I've heard lots of them.

What we really look at here at HypnoArts amongst our authors is people who can see the world in a very clear chunk. That's great.

But I'm going to ask you the three things, now, that I know people want to know the answer to because these are the things that people use as excuses, if you like.

What's the number one mistake that the people who use make in the area of ending functional using and reclaiming their life?

Hugh: The number one mistake is they have a belief that they **can't function without the substance.**

Jon: Why's that a mistake? Why do people make it?

Hugh: Because they're not recognising the impact that the using is having, psychologically, behaviourally, and physically.

They don't see that it's actually affecting their body, it's going to have a long term effect. The residual build up in the organs is going to be there over time.

Psychologically, they're going to be controlled by the monster. It may get to the point where everything revolves around them getting out of work at

4:30 so as to get to the pub by 5, or to meet their dealer at 5. They're going to do that. They're going to organise their time.

Psychologically, the whole idea of being controlled will be exactly what they want.

That whole sense of, that belief that they hold, it's a mistake to hold it. It's not the truth. It's monster talk.

Jon: The process helps them get out of that?

Hugh: The process is designed in order for them to identify what's going on.

The whole idea that the process moves them through stages, what is their monster? Name it. It's their, "Yeah, I get out of work quarter to five. I come in 15 minutes early in the morning. Some get 15 minutes late. I come in early to get out of there early and therefore can get to the dealer or the pub or home to open the bottle of wine", whatever it is.

Everything revolves around maintaining the habit, the behaviour, that they believe that they need in order to be able to function.

As long as they *believe* it, they're right.

Jon: What's the biggest myth that most often causes people who use to fail completely with ending functional using, you know, people who say, "Oh, I won't try that because..."

Jon: What's the biggest social myth, if you like.

Hugh: I think one of the biggest social messages that I come across continuously is the idea that people are powerless. That there's a powerlessness over a drug or alcohol.

And looking at that whole sense of just because they use it doesn't mean they can't stop using it. It is their choice at the end of the day.

It is a behaviour that's fuelled by something inside of themselves, the monster, which tells them that if they don't want to use, then they're going to feel crap.

Yes, they're going to feel crap, but only for a short period of time.

They do have the power, they do have the ability, they do have the capacity, you do have the energy, they do have the resilience, they do have the resources in order to be able to take power back from the monster.

So as long as they believe that they're powerless over the monster, they're right again. It's recognising that that is a myth.

Each and every one of us has the power to change our behaviours.

Jon: We do that by naming the monster, externalising it, recognising the language that it's using.

Yeah, that makes clear sense to me.

What is a simple misunderstanding that people have, because you and I both know that people are way more educated now than ever before, well, if you call Wikipedia education.

But people can look stuff up, "Oh, I'll Google that." What's the misunderstanding that people come to you with that they say, "Oh yes, of course, it's this." and it isn't?

Hugh: Yeah. A misunderstanding is the whole idea that it's not having an impact on their life. That it's not actually effecting their lives.

They have gotten to the point of accepting that the cloud of unknowing is part of their life, rather than a religious text from the middle ages.

They're not willing to see beyond that and recognise that the prefrontal lobe is affected by their use.

The prefrontal lobe is the *executive functioning* in their lives that helps them, assists them to look at, "If I do this, then that will happen."

That's gotten cloudy. Decisions and all the rest of it that they're making, they think they're making them clear headed.

That's the misunderstanding: they're not.

It's actually having an impact on the choices and the decisions and the behaviours on what they're getting, which is a big word, as you use quite a lot, the results they're getting.

The monster will be using, "You're not good enough. You're not smart enough. You're not ..." in order for people to be stuck there in that place where they don't realise, "Okay, if I did something different, I'll get different results."

Jon: So, would I be right in thinking that when you say that, what comes to me is that the monster is saying to me, "Well, I might as well use anyway because I'm not clever enough to do it anyway."

Hugh: Yeah. I would come across that quite a lot. As I said to you earlier, at the very start, that was one of the ones I used.

I wasn't smart enough to get a PHD. I wasn't smart enough to get a degree. I wasn't smart enough to even get a GCSE and all that, or whatever they're called now.

The monster used that excuse in me until I recognised that wasn't the truth.

We all have these misunderstandings that we apply to ourselves for the monster to give us the excuse, or to justify our behaviour of using. Remember, it's the monster talk, and you really do need to get clear about your monster talk that's giving you all these misunderstandings.

It's feeding into the myths and it's causing you to make mistakes of judgement.

Benefits

Jon: In the last section, we're going to look at the three major benefits that people get. I know people have reported to you, so I'm sure you can tell us some stories of actual people who have gone through the process.

When we were talking about doing this interview and doing the work, you told me the three benefits that you wanted to push more than anything else were seeing your future more clearly, taking charge of your life, and gaining peace of mind.

I've no doubt that you've got little stories that you can tell that punch home to the reader and the user that they can actually have these things.

Let's look at exactly what is the

advantage of seeing your future more clearly?

Hugh: The advantage of seeing your future more clearly is that you can actually plan ahead.

You can make decisions about what you want. You can look at the results that you want to have in your life. You can choose to make decisions that work for you and for the people you love. Now that might be that you choose to make a decision to then go for climbing the corporate ladder, or go up into management, and you clearly see that that will have a few sacrifices along the way, but you can see your future more clearly.

You can look at the challenges and opportunities with a clear head.

It's really really interesting, I worked with a young man, possibly five years ago. Worked with him, worked through the whole idea of it, and then one day I was in the office and the receptionist put a phone call through to me.

She said, "This phone call's from Australia."

I said, "Right. Okay." I said, "Hello?"

He said, "Oh, hello. It's such and such,"

I said, "But this call's from Australia."

He said, "Yeah, I'm managing a bar in Australia. Just wanted to let you know that I did everything that I needed to do. Emigrated to Australia, and got a really senior position."

That's wonderful when you hear that because for him, he wanted to get into the industry. He wanted to get into the arena of working in management within the entertainment industry, and this was his way of doing it.

It was only a stepping stone, because I asked him, "Well, how's this in relation to what you said you wanted to do?"

He said, "I'm getting there. This is a

step along the way."

When you hear stories like that and you realise, okay, he hasn't forgotten what his outcome is. He hasn't forgotten what his goal is, but he's prepared to do what he needs to do along the way to get there.

He was able to envision his whole future, see what he wanted, make clear decisions. Yes, he was faced with a few challenges, overcame them because his head was clear.

He was able to think things through. He was able to imagine his future. He had the clarity of vision to be able to turn around and say, "This is what I want and this is what I need to do to go there."

Few twists and turns along the way, but that was his choice.

Jon: The next one: what do the audience who use get most when they take charge of their own life?

Hugh: I think it's amazing when you watch someone take charge of their life and make decisions for themselves that actually take them forward.

To sit in the driver's seat of the car of your own life and be able to say, "I'm going this road," and if you decided along the way to say, "Hmm, I might take this road." You're in charge of it. You're the actual driver. You're the author whatever it is you want to do.

It's so amazing when you watch people stop giving the monster responsibility and letting the monster give them excuses and blame and victim mentality. Take charge of your life.

Choose to do what you want to do. Make the plans.

It's amazing when you watch young people, specifically young men and young women, who were hopeless and felt helpless and didn't know what to do with their life.

And you sit down with them and say, "Okay, let's look at this realistically. Let's look at what's going on here. You're believing everything this monster's telling you, and you're sitting here and you're saying to me you're hopeless, you're powerless, nothing's going to change.

Yeah, you're right if you keep doing what you're doing, but what if you could do something different? What if there was an alternative where you could take charge of your life rather than give the charge of your life to the monster and feed the monster and stop stealing, breaking into people's houses, stealing in order to feed the habit, what if you could turn that around?"

They have. They've gone into education. One person in particular, he's now got his first level diploma in health and social care.

I'm trying to think of one. It's really interesting when you watch professional people or their partners, whatever, lose their sense of self or lose their sense of responsibility in their life because of a substance.

One case in particular, the wife of a teacher who loved Christmas and Easter time because that's when all the students or parents of students would bring in bottle of wine. She loved this time because she wouldn't have to spend money buying it.

What was happening for her was the total control, her total life was being given over to, "When do I get the wine, how do I get the wine? When can I drink the wine? Drop the kids off, let's go, I can go home." You've got all of that going on. She then realised that the charge of her life, the responsibility of her life was in the hands of the monster.

Once she recognised that that was going on, she took charge of her life. It was amazing.

She went on to become one of the senior people in the parent teacher association, actually guiding and helping the parents move forward. She became a force to be reckoned with.

Before that, people didn't even know what her personality was like. It was amazing how she actually blossomed because the alcohol had dulled down her sense of who she was, of her personality. She felt worthless and undervalued by herself.

But she took charge, and everybody else began to recognise the abilities, the strengths, that she had.

Jon: So, because she took charge, **she actually got her personality back.**

Hugh: Yep.

Jon: Really read this, by the way, if you're
        reading it.

        She got her *personality back* because it
        was presumably the monster's
        personality that she was projecting to
        the world. That's huge. That's brilliant.

        Finally, the last benefit was that they
        can gain peace of mind.

Hugh: When people have actually come in
        and we're finishing up, and I ask them
        what is it that you can go away with
        now.

        For those that successfully follow the
        programme, not everybody does, but
        for those who successfully follow the
        programme and get to that point
        where they've made a new decision
        and make new choices in their life,
        they can actually sit down, in all
        honesty, in a very relaxed and
        comfortable way and say, the one

thing that they didn't realise was peace of mind.

When somebody has peace of mind, when the monster is not continuously wreaking through your mind, looking for excuses, looking for reasons, and you can sit with yourself, and you can sit with your thoughts, and you can sit with your loved ones, and you can go into board meetings and you can go into interviews, and you can go out and work with colleagues or talk to colleagues, and need a peace of mind, they will recognise it.

They will know that there is something different in you.

But it doesn't matter about them, because it matters about you. Your life has become a place you want to be in, that you don't need the substances, you don't need to do what it is you're doing in order to get away from yourself. There's a point of acceptance of self. There's a point of understanding itself, and most of all, that peace that does happen because you have changed.

You made a choice to give yourself the greatest gift, the ability to live inside your own head.

When you live inside your own head, at peace, I just wonder what that really like for you.

Jon: Have you got a little story to illustrate that for us?

Hugh: I think a really good example that we started with, and now we're coming near the end of the book is my own story. I think it's really really important that the one thing that I have given myself, and I didn't set out for it, is peace of mind.

I can sit with myself more. I can sit here and do the thing that I'm doing, knowing that inside of my head the monster isn't continuously shouting out.

My mental health is the best it could ever have been after dealing with all of that. I think it's really really important that I have taken myself to the level of my professionalism by making those choices.

I can do it with contentment and with a sense of peace of mind that will take me forward to whatever comes next and deal with that.

Jon: Thank you very much Hugh Quigley. I hope I'm not labouring the point, but I'm sure to note that our audience are professionals who use, and of course anyone else who's watching this, reading this, will find it not only interesting but useful and very very practical.

If you want more, pop along to starvethemonsterbook.com or starve the monster group on Facebook, and there's a starve the monster tutorial training online, which you can find out about when you go to the website or join the social groups.

You can also get information on the hypnoarts app, where you can join the hypnoarts.club and get this and many more. Pop along to that, and there will be links to Hugh's site.

If you want to hear Hugh speak, at one of your events, get in touch with hypnoarts and we'll arrange that for you. Thanks a lot for subscribing to our books and subscribing to our authors.

Thanks a lot to Hugh Quigley, and this is Jonathon Chase for hypnoarts, thank you.

Meet Hugh Quigley

Hugh Quigley is an expert in ending what he calls functional using, and whose accomplishments include: a Bsc (Hons) Psychology, a Post Graduate diploma in Psychotherapy & Hypnotherapy .a PhD in Philosophy, and a Distinguished Certificate in Counselling Psychology & Therapy.

Hugh Is a Drug and Alcohol Counsellor/Psychotherapist with the charity HURT London-Derry Northern Ireland, a Consultant in Development Training for Organisations all across Ireland, and runs a Private practice using hypnosis, psychotherapy and counselling.

He is a Clinical Member of UKCP – United Kingdom council For Psychotherapy and a fellow Member of the National Counselling Society and a Clinical Member of UPCA – Universities Psychotherapy & Counselling Association. He is a Winner of the R Patton Memorial Award through Centre training International school held at Queens University Belfast.

Hugh has Lectured at Liverpool John Moore's University, Masters in Education in Child Psychotherapy. Lectured for the North West

Institute foundation Degree in Counselling, and has Helped thousands get their lives back before being functional becomes dysfunctional.

On a personal level Hugh is an enthusiastic but Bad guitar player, hasn't got room to swing a cat because he Collects furniture. He Enjoys food - and especially hosting BBQ's, and is a World class solo traveler.

What most people need is instruction and encouragement from someone who has "been there and done that!" to kill your addiction thinking.

And as you can see, addiction expert Hugh Quigley is uniquely qualified to help you understand everything you need to know about reclaiming your life.

Postword

Hi there, it's Jonathan Chase.

I'm incredibly lucky because as Director and Interviewer for HypnoArts Partnership Publishing, I'm allowed to be Midwife to some awesome people's ideas, expertise and treasures being shared with the world.

Hugh Quigley is one of the most dedicated people persons you're likely to meet, which adds an edge of connection to his work most detached professionals don't have.

In starve the monster he brings decades of up close and personal experience to his work that's often lost with more evidence and theory based approaches.

Functioning addiction, or as he calls it, the Monster, is a beatable malady of modern lifestyles. Apply the strategies here because they will work for you.

Envoi: This is a 'Postword'.

Unlike a foreword I'm not here to tell you to read the book; I'm here to tell you to read it again, and again.

As with all #HypnoArtsBooks you should be able to do that on an average commute into town, definitely while you're waiting for your cancelled flight, or over a couple of lunches.

Our authors don't do fluff or fancy passages full of rhetoric, we don't do the 'bigger the book the better the content' thing.

So go back and read it again. Make notes in the margins. Fold page corners to mark the best bits. Spill coffee and tea on the cover...

READ the book and allow it to help your life change.

Enhance Your Experience. Now.

HypnoArts™ Publications

Enhancing the Experience of Life

For the most up to date information on;
Books, Audio, Courses and Video Tutorials,
Author information, links to forums
and FaceBook groups Live Author Appearances and events
download the free #HypnoArts App
from iTunes App Store or Google Play

or Visit **HypnoArts.com**
and grab your copy of our email newsletter.

We look forward to meeting you.
Jane Bregazzi. CEO HypnoArts

Notes:

Lightning Source UK Ltd.
Milton Keynes UK
UKOW01f2021111017
310832UK00004B/324/P